LAUNCH PAD
LIBRARY

ANCIENT
PEOPLES

CLAIRE FORBES

STAMPLEY

How to use this book

Cross references
Above some of the chapter titles, you will find a list of other chapters in the book that are related to the topic. Turn to these pages to find out more about each subject.

See for yourself
See-for-yourself bubbles give you the chance to test out some of the ideas in this book. They explain what you will need and what you have to do to see if an idea really works.

Quiz corner
In the quiz corner, you will find a list of questions. The answers to the quiz questions are somewhere in the same chapter. Try to answer all the questions about each subject.

Chatterboxes
Chatterboxes give you interesting facts about other things that are related to the subject.

Glossary
Difficult words are explained in the glossary on page 31. These words are in **bold** type in the book. Look them up in the glossary to find out what they mean.

Index
The index is on page 32. It is a list of important words mentioned in the book, with page numbers next to the entries. If you want to read about a subject, look it up in the index, then turn to the page number given.

Contents

Discovering the Past

Thousands of years ago, in ancient times, different groups of people lived in different parts of the world. Each group had its own way of life. Many of these peoples are no longer here today, but they have left behind some of the things they used, such as buildings, coins and masks. We can learn a lot about ancient peoples by looking at these things.

Lost treasures
Archaeologists are people who dig up and study objects to find out how ancient peoples lived. They are like history detectives. They cannot always build a complete picture of the people they are studying because many objects, such as those made of wood or cloth, have rotted away.

▶ This ancient mask has lasted because it is made of a metal that does not rot away.

▲ This metal coin was used about two thousand years ago by ancient Romans.

▶ These maps show the places where the ancient peoples in this book lived.

Five thousand years ago, ancient Egyptians lived by the Nile River in northern Africa.

Over two thousand years ago, ancient Greeks lived by the Mediterranean Sea.

▼ These stone **columns** and statues are part of the remains of an amazing Mayan city, Chichen-Itza, that was built in Mexico in ancient times.

Quiz Corner

- Name two things that ancient peoples used that we can still see today.

- What do archaeologists study?

- Where did the Maya live?

Two thousand years ago, the Romans lived in the country we now call Italy.

About three thousand years ago, the ancient Chinese lived in east Asia.

Over one thousand years ago, the Maya lived in Mexico and Central America.

Over one thousand years ago, the Vikings lived in northern Europe.

look at: Egyptian Beliefs, page 8

Ancient Egypt

About 5,000 years ago, the **civilization** of ancient Egypt stretched along the banks of the Nile River. The ancient Egyptians lived by the Nile because the river flooded every year, bringing water to fields where they could grow food. The ancient Egyptian civilization lasted for about 3,000 years. During this time, people farmed the land, built towns and developed their own way of writing.

▲ In ancient Egyptian writing, words and sentences were made up of pictures which we call hieroglyphs.

Egyptian houses
Most ancient Egyptians lived in small, square houses built with mud bricks. Each house had small windows that let in a little light but kept out the heat of the sun. At night, the family slept on the flat roof, where it was cool.

▶ The busiest places in a town were markets where people did not pay with money but swapped goods with one another.

SEE FOR YOURSELF

Try writing using pictures. You can copy the examples below or make up your own. Try to make up enough picture words to write a secret message.

bird eye boat water

School and games

Most ancient Egyptian children did not go to school. Boys worked with their fathers and girls helped their mothers at home. In their free time, children played games such as leapfrog and tug-of-war.

▲ Ancient Egyptian children played with toys such as this wooden horse. They also played with dolls and balls made of clay.

Quiz Corner

● Which river was important to the ancient Egyptians?

● Why did ancient Egyptian houses have small windows?

● What games did ancient Egyptian children play?

Egyptian Beliefs

Religion was very important to the ancient Egyptians. They worshipped and prayed to many different **gods**. The ancient Egyptians believed that they would go to a new world when they died. They were buried with things they might need for this new world, such as food, weapons, tools and furniture.

Egyptian kings

The kings who ruled ancient Egypt were called pharaohs. A pharaoh was very powerful and treated like a god by the Egyptian people. When a pharaoh died, he was often buried inside an enormous tomb called a pyramid.

▼ Pyramids were built from heavy blocks of stone and took many years to finish.

Building a pyramid

Workers began building a pharaoh's pyramid long before he died. They dragged heavy blocks of stone up a ramp to the building site, using ropes and logs. Then each stone was put into place.

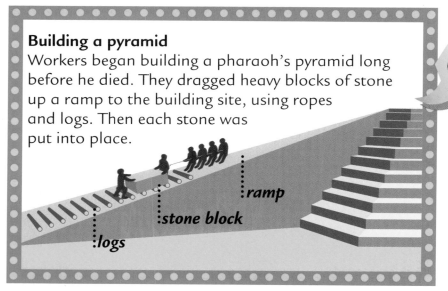

ramp

stone block

logs

CHATTERBOX

One of the most important **goddesses** to the ancient Egyptians was Isis. Egyptian women believed that Isis would protect and care for them in their daily life.

8

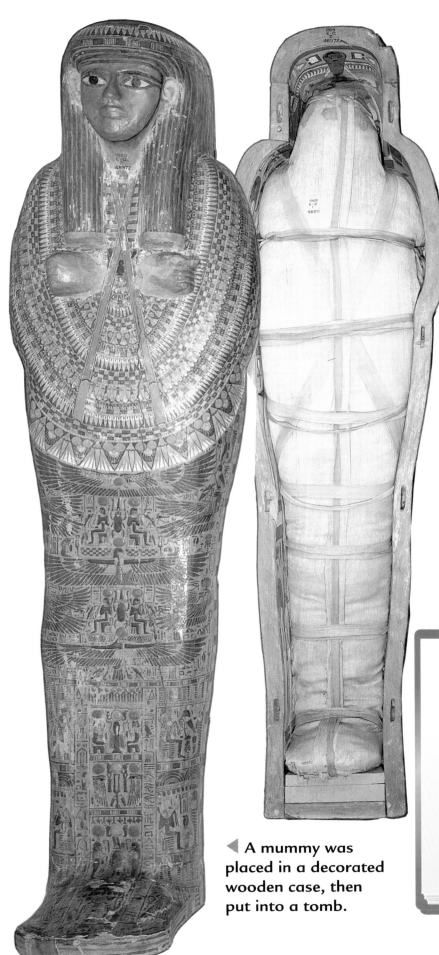

Mummies

Ancient Egyptians believed they would need their bodies in the next life. When pharaohs and rich people died, their bodies were dried, preserved with salts, and wrapped in bandages to keep them from rotting. Bodies kept like this are called mummies.

Egyptian cats

Cats were holy animals to the ancient Egyptians. When a pet cat died, the owner shaved off his own eyebrows to show how sad he was.

▶ Mummies of cats have been found buried in the tombs of ancient Egyptians.

◀ A mummy was placed in a decorated wooden case, then put into a tomb.

Quiz Corner

● What were ancient Egyptian kings called?

● Which animals were holy to the ancient Egyptians?

● Where were Egyptian kings often buried?

9

look at: Life in Greece, page 12

Ancient Greece

Over 2,000 years ago, the land of Greece was divided into **city-states**. Each city-state had its own city, farmland, army and laws. The city-state of Athens was famous for learning and **drama**, while Sparta was famous for its army. The ancient Greeks were the first people to **vote** for their rulers.

Greek plays

The first plays were put on in Athens. They were performed during religious festivals in huge open-air theaters. All the parts of the play were acted by men, who wore masks to show different characters and emotions.

SEE FOR YOURSELF

Make your own Greek mask using a white paper plate. Ask an adult to help you cut out the eyes, mouth and nose, and to make a small hole at each side. Paint your mask. Then thread elastic through the small holes and tie a knot at each side.

A group of actors called the chorus explained what was happening in the play.

School

Greek boys went to school from the age of seven to fifteen. Since parents had to pay for their schooling, boys from poorer families spent fewer years in school than did boys from richer families. Greek girls did not go to school. At home, their mothers taught them to cook, spin and weave.

CHATTERBOX

In Athens, schoolboys were taught reading, writing, arithmetic, sports, poetry and music. But school life was different in the city-state of Sparta. Boys were taught to fight, steal and lie in order to make them cunning soldiers.

▲ Schoolboys did not have paper and pencils. They used a pointed stick, called a stylus, to scratch into a layer of wax in a wooden frame.

Work

Many ancient Greek men were farmers or craftsmen. Women and young girls took care of the house, prepared food and made clothes. Rich Greek men and women kept **slaves** to help them with their work. Greek women and slaves had no say in how their city-state was run.

Sometimes Greek plays lasted all day, so the actors had to have good memories.

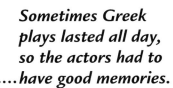

◀ During a play, the audience sat on steps around the stage. Poor people paid less than rich people for the same seats.

Quiz Corner

● Which city-state was famous for its army?

● Which subjects did schoolboys in Athens study?

● Who explained what was happening in an ancient Greek play?

look at: Ancient Greece, page 10

Life in Greece

The ancient Greeks are famous for many things. They carved beautiful statues and built huge stone buildings and **temples**. They also invented a sporting contest called the Olympic Games, which still takes place today. We have learned many things from the ancient Greeks, including ideas about science, **government**, math and medicine.

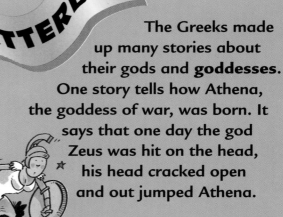

CHATTERBOX

The Greeks made up many stories about their gods and **goddesses**. One story tells how Athena, the goddess of war, was born. It says that one day the god Zeus was hit on the head, his head cracked open and out jumped Athena.

Olympic Games

Every four years, the Olympic Games took place in Olympia on the west coast of Greece. The games were held in honor of the Greek **god** Zeus. People came from all over Greece to take part in events such as boxing, running, wrestling and javelin throwing.

▶ This picture from a vase shows a man riding a **chariot** pulled by horses. Chariot races were held at the ancient Olympic Games.

Winning the Olympics
On the last day of the Olympics, winners were given a crown woven from the leaves of olive trees. There was also a big feast and a huge celebration.

12

▲ In one Olympic event, men threw a discus, or bronze disk, as far as they could.

Greek columns

Buildings in ancient Greece often had tall, straight **columns**. Today, only a few ancient Greek buildings are left, but buildings in a similar style have been built in many towns around the world.

▲ This Greek temple is called the Parthenon. It was built in Athens for the goddess Athena.

Quiz Corner

- Name three things for which the ancient Greeks are famous.

- Which sporting contest did the ancient Greeks invent?

- For what goddess was the Parthenon built?

look at: Life in Greece, page 12; The Roman Army, page 16

Ancient Rome

People could collect drinking water from fountains in the street.

About 2,000 years ago, the Romans ruled many lands around the Mediterranean Sea, including the country we now call Italy. These lands made up the Roman **Empire**. The Romans built many towns and cities in their empire. The largest and most important city was Rome.

Most Romans washed in public bathhouses.

People watched contests and other entertainment in huge arenas.

Roman houses

Many rich Romans lived in large town houses with gardens. **Slaves** looked after everything. Poor Romans lived in tiny apartments, without running water or kitchens.

◀ Mosaics were made out of tiny pieces of colored stone. Rich Romans decorated their floors with them.

SEE FOR YOURSELF

Here is an easy way to make a mosaic. Draw the outline of a picture on a piece of stiff paper. Using different colors of paper cut many, many small squares. Glue the squares to the paper following your outline.

▲ Roman towns were full of grand buildings, such as **temples**, theaters and public baths.

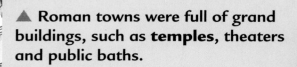

*People gathered in the **forum**, or town square, to have meetings and to buy and sell things.*

*Roman temples held statues of **gods**. People gave gifts to the gods hoping for good luck in return.*

▲ The Romans built bridges to carry water from lakes to the towns. This bridge carried water to the city of Nîmes, France.

Carrying water

Fresh water was transported through pipes that lay in the tops of aqueducts, or water bridges. In town, sewer pipes which had been laid under the streets carried away dirty, used water.

Quiz Corner

- Why did Roman people gather in the forum?

- Where did most Romans bathe?

- How did the Romans bring water from lakes to towns?

look at: Ancient Rome, page 14

The Roman Army

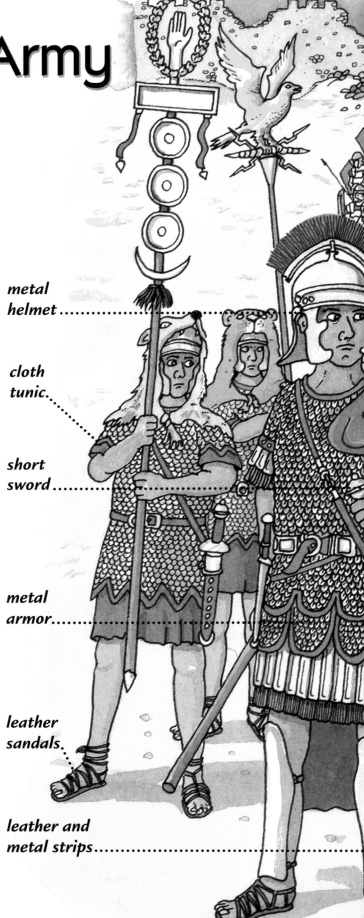

The Roman army was the most successful army of ancient times. It protected the **Empire** and made sure that everyone living there followed Roman laws. The army was made up of trained soldiers from all over the Empire. The soldiers built roads that linked the towns and cities in the Empire.

Foot soldiers

Most Roman soldiers traveled on foot. Each one carried a short sword, a dagger, a spear and a shield. A soldier wore a helmet on his head and metal armor over his chest for protection. Strips of leather covered with metal hung from his belt. When he walked, these strips clanked loudly and helped to frighten his enemies.

metal helmet.............

cloth tunic...

short sword.........

metal armor.............

leather sandals...

leather and metal strips..........................

Under a shell

In battle, soldiers locked their shields together to make a kind of shell around themselves. This protected them from rocks and spears thrown by enemies.

Over the walls

Soldiers used wooden towers to break into enemy cities. They climbed up the towers and fought their way over the city walls. Soldiers also fired rocks from giant catapults to knock down the walls.

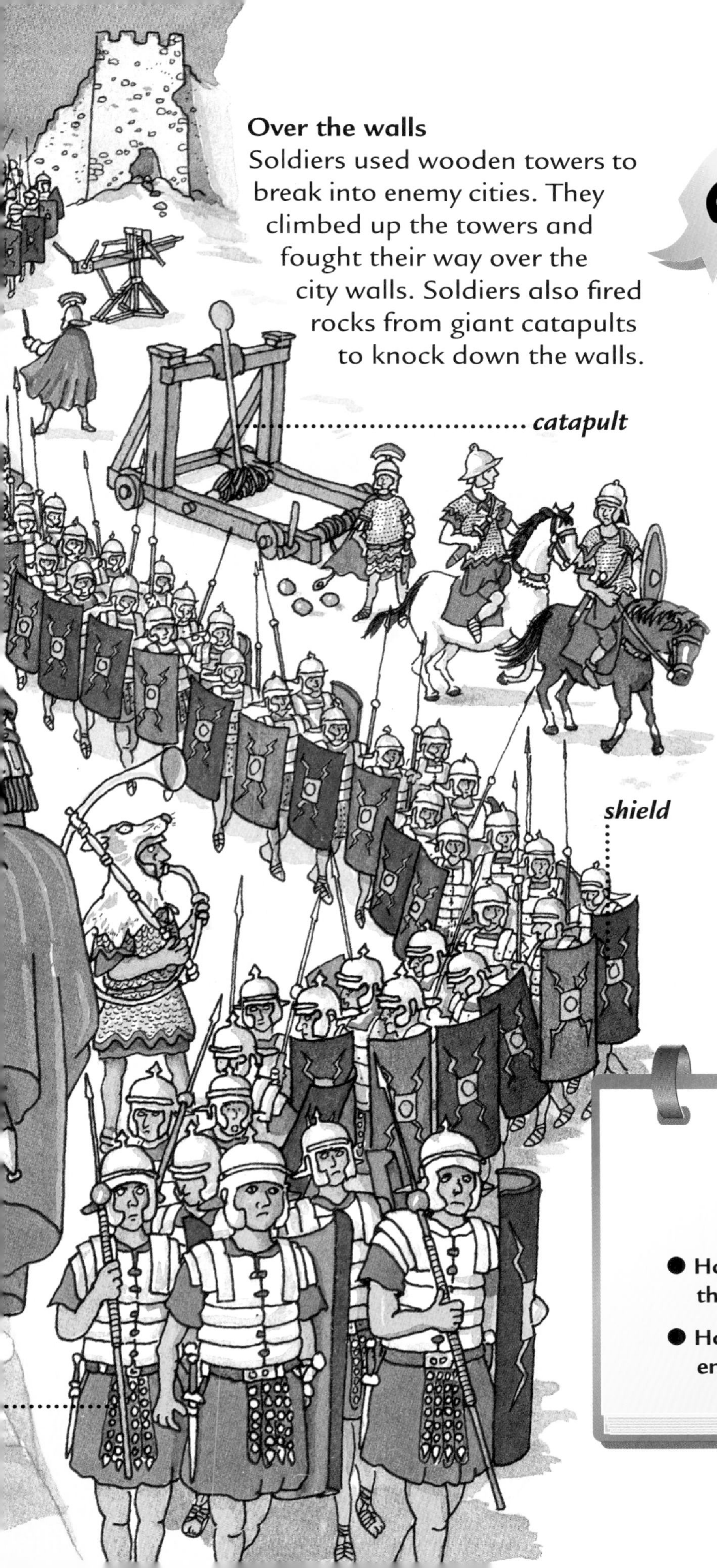

.... *catapult*

shield

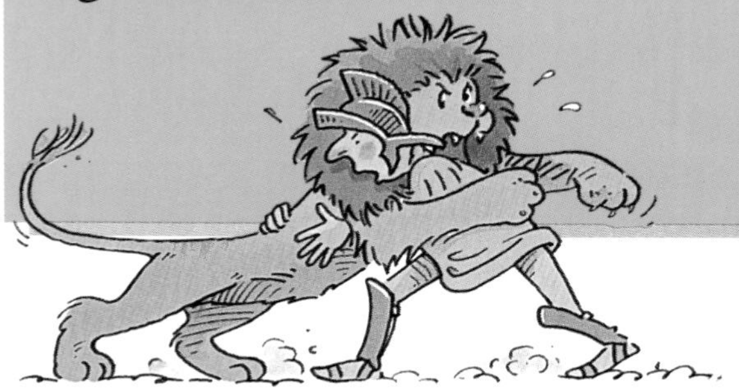

Soldiers' backpacks

When foot soldiers were marching, they carried everything they needed in backpacks. Inside, they had cooking pots, bedding and enough food to last for up to three days.

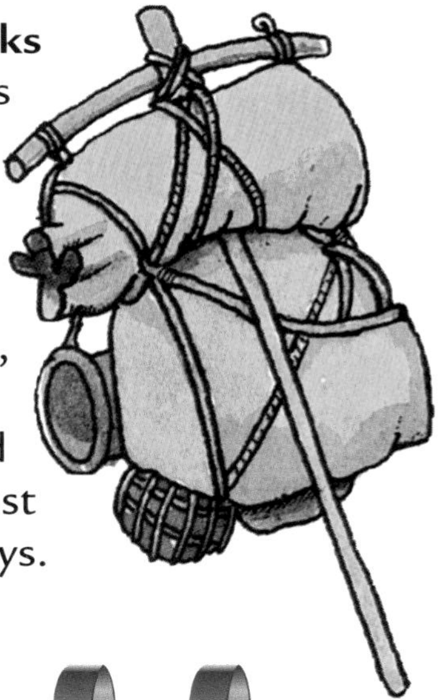

Quiz Corner

● How did groups of Roman soldiers use their shields to protect themselves?

● How did Roman soldiers enter enemy towns?

17

look at: Chinese Inventions, page 20

Ancient China

Until a few hundred years ago, the way of life in China had changed very little. Most people were farmers who lived in the countryside. They worked hard growing food. Others worked as craftsmen or **merchants**. A ruler called the emperor **governed** the country with the help of officials.

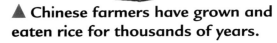

▲ **Chinese farmers have grown and eaten rice for thousands of years.**

Chinese food
Farmers were important because they grew food for the many thousands of people who lived in ancient China. Most people ate vegetables, millet and rice, but the emperor and other rich people often ate much more expensive food, such as shark fins and bear paws.

▶ **Jugglers and musicians entertained the emperor at feasts.**

Family life
In most Chinese families, children, parents and grandparents all lived in the same house. Parents and elders were very strict with children, and wives were expected to obey their husbands.

CHATTERBOX

The ancient Chinese believed that overhanging roofs would keep bad spirits out of the building. Many roof tiles were also painted to scare away evil spirits.

Tomb treasures

The ancient Chinese believed in life after death. When an emperor died, he was buried with models of horses, servants and **chariots**. He hoped that these models would help him in his new life.

▲ When China's first emperor died, he was buried with 7,000 life-size terracotta models of soldiers to protect him.

Quiz Corner

● Why did the ancient Chinese have overhanging roofs?

● By whom were the people of ancient China ruled?

● Why were China's emperors buried with models of horses, servants and chariots?

look at: Ancient China, page 18

Chinese Inventions

The ancient Chinese were amazing inventors. They invented paper and developed a way of printing books using wooden blocks. Other countries did not develop these things until hundreds of years later. The Chinese also invented wheelbarrows, umbrellas and playing cards.

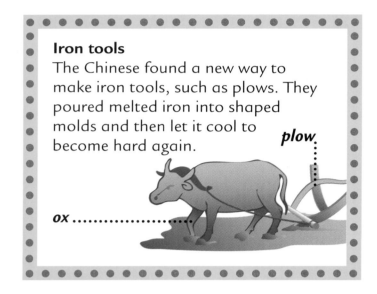

Iron tools
The Chinese found a new way to make iron tools, such as plows. They poured melted iron into shaped molds and then let it cool to become hard again.

plow

ox

▲ The first fireworks were made by the Chinese. They used gunpowder to launch the fireworks into the air.

Land of silk
The Chinese made a fine cloth called silk. They **traded** silk with other people in Asia. Chinese silk was so popular that the Romans called China Serica, which means "land of silk."

▶ Rich people wore beautiful silk robes. This robe belonged to the wife of an emperor.

Enemy attacks
The Great Wall was built to protect China from attacks by invaders from the north. It took thousands of people hundreds of years to build it.

▼ The Great Wall of China is the longest wall in the world. In the past, guards walked along the path on the top of the wall and lit warning fires if enemies came near.

Quiz Corner

- Name three things that the ancient Chinese invented.
- Why was ancient China called the "land of silk"?
- Why did the ancient Chinese build the Great Wall of China?

look at: Life in Mayan Times, page 24

The Maya

Over 1,000 years ago, an ancient people called the Maya made their home in Mexico and Central America. They lived in **city-states**, which were made up of a city, nearby villages and farmland. The Maya were expert **astronomers**. They also developed their own way of counting and writing.

Mayan cities

The Maya built great stone cities with huge pyramids, palaces and **temples**. They often covered their temples with shiny white plaster or painted them bright red. Sometimes Mayan cities went to war with each other. When enemies were captured, they were made into **slaves**.

▲ Mayan temples were built on top of high, flat-topped pyramids in the center of the city. These temples are in the ancient city of Uxmal in Mexico.

Pleasing the gods

The Maya worshipped many different **gods** and prayed to them every day for help with their daily tasks. They also held **ceremonies** for their gods. Sometimes a ball game called pok-a-tok was played at these ceremonies.

▶ Pok-a-tok was played on a ball court inside the city. Players used only their elbows or hips to hit a rubber ball through a stone ring at one end of the court.

◀ Today, only a few Mayan books are left. They are kept in museums.

Mayan books

The Maya wrote on long strips of tree bark, which they folded into pages and made into books. The covers of the books were made from jaguar skins. The Maya wrote with brushes or feathers dipped in colored inks.

Quiz Corner

● How did the Maya make books?

● What kinds of buildings were in Mayan cities?

● On what did the Maya write?

● What was pok-a-tok?

look at: The Maya, page 22

Life in Mayan Times

Most Maya were farmers who grew crops for food and raised bees for honey. They also hunted animals to eat. The Maya lived in simple huts. Girls stayed at home with their mothers and learned how to take care of a family. Mayan boys were sent away to special houses, where they learned about fighting and war.

avocado

Mayan food
The Maya grew corn, beans, chili peppers, and fruit such as papayas and avocados. They also planted cacao trees, which gave them cocoa beans for making chocolate. Cocoa beans were sometimes used as money.

papaya

chili pepper

Growing corn
Corn was the most important food for the Maya. They ate it as part of nearly every meal. For breakfast, they ate a thin porridge made from ground corn. Field-workers ate corn dumplings.

Mayan homelife

Mayan women prepared food and made clothes at home. They also grew crops. Mayan men went hunting, using bows and arrows to kill large animals such as deer.

◀ Mayan women wove cotton on tall, wooden looms. They ground corn into flour using special grinding stones.

Mayan calendars

The Maya had several **calendars** to help them count days and years. They believed that some days on the calendars were unlucky. On these days, the Maya tried to do as little work as possible.

▲ This statue has pictures of animals and **gods** carved on it to show important events in Mayan times.

CHATTERBOX

The Maya believed that the sun and the planet Venus played an important part in their lives. They thought that the position Venus was in when a child was born helped shape his or her character.

Mayan makeup

To make themselves look beautiful, the Maya filed their front teeth into sharp points and filled the gaps with pieces of a hard green stone called jade. Married men and women also decorated their bodies with tattoos from the waist up. Unmarried men and warriors painted their bodies black. Unmarried women painted their bodies red.

Quiz Corner

● What did the Maya eat as part of nearly every meal?

● What did the Maya do on unlucky days?

● How did the Maya make themselves look beautiful?

The Vikings

Over 1,000 years ago, the Vikings lived in a part of northern Europe called **Scandinavia**. Their lands were crowded, so they built wooden ships and sailed to other countries. Some Vikings were warriors and attacked these countries, but many were traders who set up new towns in the places where they settled.

◀ Rich Viking sailors wore iron helmets such as this one. Poorer Vikings had to make do with leather caps.

Warships

Large Viking ships were called longships. They were light and traveled quickly. Longships could sail up rivers, as well as across seas. Each longship had a sail, oars for rowing and a wider, heavier oar at the back for steering. Inside the ship were boxes in which Viking sailors kept weapons such as swords and axes.

▶ The front of Viking ships were usually carved into the shape of a bird, serpent or dragon.

Land travel

In summer, Vikings rode on horses or in carts pulled by horses or oxen. In winter when snow covered the ground, they traveled on sleds, skis or ice skates.

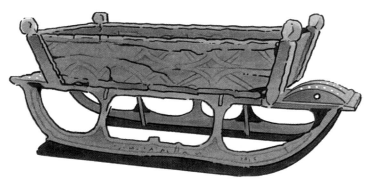

▲ Sleds were used to pull heavy loads, such as firewood, over the icy ground.

Crossing the ocean

The Vikings were brave explorers. They were the first people to sail across the Atlantic Ocean from Europe to North America. The Vikings made their homes in many of the places to which they traveled, including Iceland, Greenland and Britain.

Quiz Corner

● From where did the Vikings come?

● In which places did the Vikings settle?

● Name two Viking weapons.

● In winter, how did Vikings travel over land?

look at: The Vikings, page 26

Viking Life

Vikings were farmers and fishermen as well as sailors. They grew food, hunted wild animals for their meat and skins and caught fish to eat. They also raised sheep and cattle. When the men were away at sea, women ran the farms and wove cloth for sails, blankets and clothes.

Writing and storytelling

The Viking alphabet had sixteen letters called runes. Each rune was made mostly of straight lines, which were easier than curved lines to carve into wood or stone. The Vikings used the runes to write messages. Long stories were usually learned by heart and told aloud rather than written down.

▲ Most Viking houses were made of wood, but some were made from stone or dirt.

Housing

Viking families lived in long houses that had only one room and no windows. A fire was kept burning in the middle of the room for heat and light and for cooking food such as stew. Most people slept and ate on benches around the edges of the room. Outside the house were workshops for making tools and sheds where animals were kept.

▲ This ancient Viking stone has runes carved within a border around its edges.

Sagas

Viking children were taught at home. They were told long stories, or sagas, about the adventures of the **gods** or of great Viking heroes. Storytellers traveled around telling sagas aloud at feasts and festivals. They were especially popular on cold, winter nights, when everyone sat inside the house around the fire.

SEE FOR YOURSELF

Viking clothes had no buttons, zippers or snaps. They were held together by brooches and belts. Look at your clothes and see how many different ways there are of fastening them.

Quiz Corner

- Who took care of the farm when the Viking men were away?
- How many rooms were there in a Viking house?
- What are the letters of the Viking alphabet called?

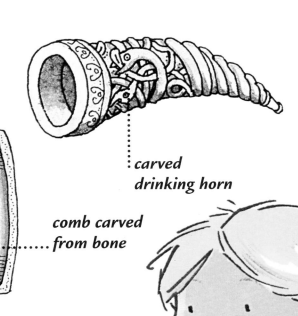

carved drinking horn

comb carved from bone

Viking crafts

The Vikings were skilled craftsmen who carved and decorated all kinds of materials. They made combs, spoons and ice skates from animal bones, and tents and sleeping bags from animal skins. Jewelry, such as rings, was made from gold, silver and bronze. Necklaces had amber, glass or jet beads. The Vikings also made pots on pottery wheels.

silver spoon

▶ Vikings enjoyed playing and listening to music. This girl is playing a carved wooden pipe.

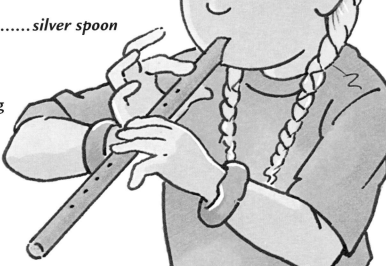

Amazing facts

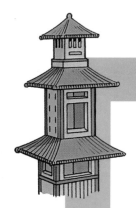

● Viking soldiers believed that they would go to a place called Valhalla if they died in battle. Valhalla was a type of paradise where they could fight all day and hold feasts all night.

☆ *The Great Pyramid was built in Egypt in ancient times, but most of it is still standing today. It is made from over two million blocks of stone.*

● At the funerals of some rich ancient Greeks, people were paid to cry for the dead. Their tears were collected and kept in an amphora, a kind of jar.

☆ *The ancient Egyptians did not have knives or forks, so they ate with their fingers. A pharaoh had a servant to wash his hands between each course of a meal.*

● Most Roman men did not grow beards. But when Emperor Hadrian grew a beard, other men in Roman lands copied him and grew beards, too.

☆ *In ancient China, men and women grew their hair long and wore it in a bun on top of their heads. They cut it only when a member of their family died.*

● Romans flavored their food with liquamen, which was made from the insides of fish. The fish were mixed with salt water and left to rot in the sun.

☆ *The Maya thought that flat heads and crossed eyes were beautiful. A baby's head was strapped between two boards to flatten it. Older children had a bead dangled in front of their eyes to make them cross-eyed.*

● The ancient Greeks told tales of the minotaur, a monster with a bull's head and a man's body, which lived in a maze and ate people.

☆ *There is an old Chinese legend, or story, that says that the Great Wall of China is not a wall at all, but a huge dragon that turned to stone.*

Glossary

astronomer A person who studies the moon, the sun, the stars and the planets.

calendar A chart that shows the days, weeks and months in a year.

ceremony A special act to mark an occasion.

chariot A two-wheeled cart that is usually pulled by horses.

city-state A city and the surrounding farms, villages and houses ruled by it.

civilization A group of people with its own set of laws and customs.

column A tall, round post used as support or decoration for a building.

drama A play that is acted on a stage.

empire A group of lands or countries under one ruler.

forum The main square of an ancient Roman town. Important business took place there.

god/goddess A being or object that people worship and believe to have great powers.

govern To rule a country.

government The group of people in charge of a country.

merchant A person who buys, sells or swaps goods to make money.

Scandinavia The name for an area of land including Norway, Sweden and Denmark.

slave A servant who is treated as property and whose rights have been taken away.

temple A building in which the worship of a **god** takes place.

trade To buy, sell or swap goods.

vote To choose something or someone, such as a law or a ruler.

Index

Published in the USA by
C.D. Stampley Enterprises, Inc.,
Charlotte, NC, USA.
Created by Two-Can Publishing Ltd.,
London. English language edition
©Two-Can Publishing Ltd, 1997

Text: Claire Forbes
Research: Rachel Wright
Consultants: Margaret Mulvihill,
Tim Wood
Watercolor artwork: Peter Kent,
Stuart Trotter
Computer artwork: D Oliver

Editorial Director: Jane Wilsher
Art Director: Carole Orbell
Production Director: Lorraine Estelle
Project Manager: Eljay Yildirim
Editors: Belinda Webber,
Deborah Kespert
Assistant Editors: Julia Hillyard,
Claire Yude
Co-edition Editor: Leila Peerun
Photo research:
Dipika Palmer-Jenkins

ISBN: 0-915741-82-2

Photographic credits: Britstock-IFA
(West Stock Montgomery) p19, p21;
Bruce Coleman (M.P.L. Fogden) p5;
C.M. Dixon p28r; e.t.archive p28l; Steve
Gorton p24; Michael Holford p8, p13r,
p15, (British Museum) p4bl, p6, p7, p9,
p12-13c, (Bardo Museum, Tunis) p14;
Tony Stone Images p20l; Werner
Forman Archive (British Museum) front
cover, (Egyptian Museum, Cairo) p4tr,
(Metropolitan Museum of Art, N.Y.)
p20r, (Museum of Anthropology,
Mexico) p25, (Statens Historiska
Museum, Stockholm) p26; Zefa p22.